2018
Get Up and Go Diar

ISBN 978191092120

Published in Ireland t
GET UP AND GO PUBLICATIONS LTD
Email: info@getupandgodiary.com
www.getupandgodiary.com

Compiled by Eileen Forrestal
Graphic design by Nuala Redmond
Illustrations by John Shanks
Printed in Ireland by GPS Colour Graphics.

GetUpandGo

Designed for Youth
Inspired by Life

May your coming year be filled with magic and dreams and good
madness. I hope you read some fine books and kiss someone who
thinks you're wonderful, and don't forget to make some art —
write or draw or build or sing or live as only you can. And I hope,
somewhere in the next year, you surprise yourself.

Neil Gaiman

THIS DIARY CONTAINS THOUGHTS ABOUT...

SPORT

BEING POPULAR

Light

Life

love

Caring

Literature

Cool

humour

The miracle of your mind

travel

FUN

VALUES

family

Poetry

friendship

kindness

Romance

patience

luck

HAPPINESS

Music

RESPONSIBILITY

GOALS

art

drama

You have a very powerful brain, if you use it positively it can do amazing things for you

Calendar 2018

JANUARY

Mon	Tue	Wed	Thu	Fri	Sat	Sun
1	2	3	4	5	6	7
8	9	10	11	12	13	14
15	16	17	18	19	20	21
22	23	24	25	26	27	28
29	30	31				

FEBRUARY

Mon	Tue	Wed	Thu	Fri	Sat	Sun
			1	2	3	4
5	6	7	8	9	10	11
12	13	14	15	16	17	18
19	20	21	22	23	24	25
26	27	28				

MARCH

Mon	Tue	Wed	Thu	Fri	Sat	Sun
			1	2	3	4
5	6	7	8	9	10	11
12	13	14	15	16	17	18
19	20	21	22	23	24	25
26	27	28	29	30	31	

APRIL

Mon	Tue	Wed	Thu	Fri	Sat	Sun
						1
2	3	4	5	6	7	8
9	10	11	12	13	14	15
16	17	18	19	20	21	22
23	24	25	26	27	28	29
30						

MAY

Mon	Tue	Wed	Thu	Fri	Sat	Sun
	1	2	3	4	5	6
7	8	9	10	11	12	13
14	15	16	17	18	19	20
21	22	23	24	25	26	27
28	29	30	31			

JUNE

Mon	Tue	Wed	Thu	Fri	Sat	Sun
				1	2	3
4	5	6	7	8	9	10
11	12	13	14	15	16	17
18	19	20	21	22	23	24
25	26	27	28	29	30	

JULY

Mon	Tue	Wed	Thu	Fri	Sat	Sun
						1
2	3	4	5	6	7	8
9	10	11	12	13	14	15
16	17	18	19	20	21	22
23	24	25	26	27	28	29
30	31					

AUGUST

Mon	Tue	Wed	Thu	Fri	Sat	Sun
		1	2	3	4	5
6	7	8	9	10	11	12
13	14	15	16	17	18	19
20	21	22	23	24	25	26
27	28	29	30	31		

SEPTEMBER

Mon	Tue	Wed	Thu	Fri	Sat	Sun
					1	2
3	4	5	6	7	8	9
10	11	12	13	14	15	16
17	18	19	20	21	22	23
24	25	26	27	28	29	30

OCTOBER

Mon	Tue	Wed	Thu	Fri	Sat	Sun
1	2	3	4	5	6	7
8	9	10	11	12	13	14
15	16	17	18	19	20	21
22	23	24	25	26	27	28
29	30	31				

NOVEMBER

Mon	Tue	Wed	Thu	Fri	Sat	Sun
			1	2	3	4
5	6	7	8	9	10	11
12	13	14	15	16	17	18
19	20	21	22	23	24	25
26	27	28	29	30		

DECEMBER

Mon	Tue	Wed	Thu	Fri	Sat	Sun
					1	2
3	4	5	6	7	8	9
10	11	12	13	14	15	16
17	18	19	20	21	22	23
24	25	26	27	28	29	30
31						

Our lives are storybooks that we write for ourselves, wonderfully illustrated by the people we meet.

This Diary Belongs To: _____

Address: _____

Telephone: _____

Email: _____

EMERGENCY TELEPHONE NUMBERS

_____

_____

_____

Your diary contains 148 pages of inspiration!
Enjoy every page!

Follow us on **Facebook:** Get Up and Go Diary for Teens and Young People;
Twitter: @getupandgo1; **Instagram:** @getupandgodiary

GOALS

FOR JANUARY

Things I want to accomplish

_____

Results I intend to achieve

_____

> Great leaders are almost always great simplifiers, who can cut through argument, debate and doubt to offer a solution everybody can understand.
> _Colin Powell_

Subjects I want to study

_____

Skills I want to learn

_____

My dreams

JANUARY

Tell me, what is it you plan to do with your one wild and precious life?

Mary Oliver

99% of the failures come from people who have the habit of making **excuses.**

George Washington

MONDAY 1 2018!!

This year starts today

YOUR CHOICE

If you think you're a winner, you'll win.
If you dare to step out you'll succeed.
Believe in your heart, have a purpose to start,
Aim to help others in need.

Thoughts of faith must replace every doubt.
Words of courage and you cannot fail.
If you stumble and fall, rise and stand tall.
You determine the course that you sail.

If you have an idea, go for it. Lots of people doubt, but if you are really passionate about your idea and what you're giving to the world, it will show.

TUESDAY 2

Wherever you are, be here now

WEDNESDAY 3

Life happens out there

THURSDAY 4

Stay calm and carry on

There are two ways to live your life — one is as though nothing is a miracle; the other is as though everything is a miracle.

Albert Einstein

JANUARY

This is my wish for you: comfort on difficult days, smiles when sadness intrudes, rainbows to follow the clouds, laughter to kiss your lips, sunsets to warm your heart, hugs when spirits sag, beauty for your eyes to see, friendships to brighten your being, faith so that you can believe, confidence for when you doubt, courage to know yourself, patience to accept the truth, love to complete your life.

Ralph Waldo Emerson

FRIDAY 5

Love your life

SATURDAY 6

The loving are worthy of being loved

SUNDAY 7

Be kind and considerate

Teachers open the doors, but you must enter by yourself.

Chinese proverb

> In matters of style, swim with the current; in matters of principle, stand like a rock.

Thomas Jefferson

You have a gift.
It's the gift of a mind that is capable
of truly remarkable endeavors.
Miraculous, even!
You see, your IQ doesn't define you.
Your salary doesn't define you.
Likewise, your level of fitness,
your current career position,
and your number of friends don't define who you are either.
Rather, greatness exists within you.
Incredible ability is there, just waiting to be tapped.
You're on the cusp of realising fantastic achievements.
And it's all within your mind – it's all within your reach!
So the question has never been "do you have the skills, the talent,
and the ability to be great?"
The question is: "how will you begin to reveal your greatness,
your gift, right now?"

Parents are special, so guard them with care.
Cherish and love them, whilst they are still there.
Cheer them and comfort their pains and their fears,
Help them and show them your thanks through the years.
Give them your patience as they both grow old,
For the love you have shared, is more precious than gold.

JANUARY

Talent wins games, but teamwork and intelligence wins championships.

Michael Jordan

MONDAY 8

Be positive and encouraging to your friends

TUESDAY 9

If you want the result you must take the action

WEDNESDAY 10

Everything begins in the imagination

THURSDAY 11

Triumph is just an 'upmh' added to a little 'try'

If you want to be happy, you have to be happy on purpose. Don't just wait to see what kind of day you will have, decide what kind of day you will have. It's your day!

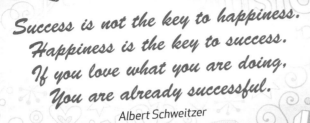

Success is not the key to happiness.
Happiness is the key to success.
If you love what you are doing,
You are already successful.

Albert Schweitzer

FRIDAY 12

Every journey starts with a first step

SATURDAY 13

Learn to dance with life

SUNDAY 14

Life is a school and we are here to learn

Believe me, human potential can be explored.
When you think it's too late,
be careful you don't let that
become your excuse for giving up.
No one can keep you from success
except yourself.
When it's time to shine,
be the brightest.

Wang Deshun

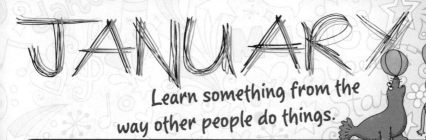

JANUARY

Learn something from the way other people do things.

MONDAY 15

Spend time with enthusiastic people

> Anyone who doesn't take the truth seriously in small matters cannot be trusted in larger ones either.
>
> *Albert Einstein*

TUESDAY 16

Everyone just wants to be heard

WEDNESDAY 17

He who gossips to you will gossip about you

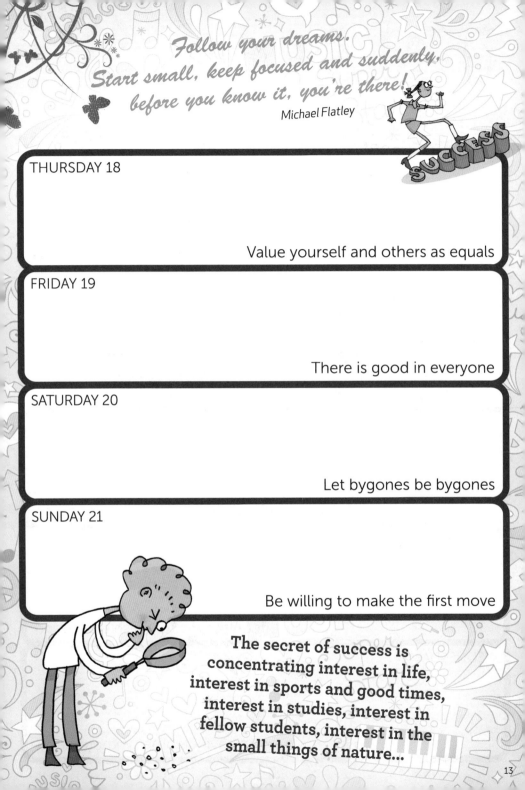

Follow your dreams.
Start small, keep focused and suddenly,
before you know it, you're there!
Michael Flatley

THURSDAY 18

Value yourself and others as equals

FRIDAY 19

There is good in everyone

SATURDAY 20

Let bygones be bygones

SUNDAY 21

Be willing to make the first move

The secret of success is
concentrating interest in life,
interest in sports and good times,
interest in studies, interest in
fellow students, interest in the
small things of nature...

JANUARY

Far and away the best prize that life has to offer is the chance to work hard at work worth doing.
Theodore Roosevelt

MONDAY 22

Think yourself confident; act with confidence

TUESDAY 23

It takes time to polish a diamond

WEDNESDAY 24

Not much worth having comes without effort

I don't know what your destiny will be, but one thing I know: The only ones among you who will be truly happy are those who have sought and found how to serve.

The most important thing is to enjoy your life — to be happy — it's all that matters.

Audrey Hepburn

The meaning of life is to give meaning to your life.

William H McRaven

THURSDAY 25

Don't argue with the facts

FRIDAY 26

Respect your friends

SATURDAY 27

Take some time to figure out what you really want

SUNDAY 28

You must work to succeed and play when you get there

JANUARY

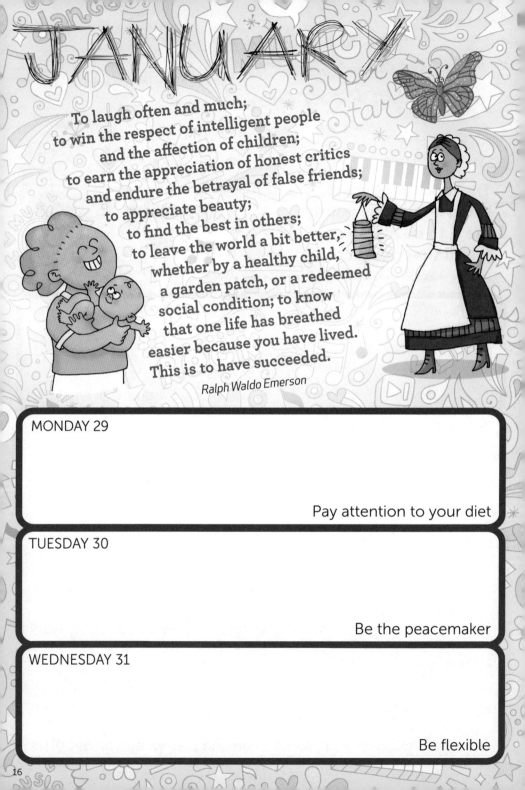

To laugh often and much;
to win the respect of intelligent people
and the affection of children;
to earn the appreciation of honest critics
and endure the betrayal of false friends;
to appreciate beauty;
to find the best in others;
to leave the world a bit better,
whether by a healthy child,
a garden patch, or a redeemed
social condition; to know
that one life has breathed
easier because you have lived.
This is to have succeeded.

Ralph Waldo Emerson

MONDAY 29

Pay attention to your diet

TUESDAY 30

Be the peacemaker

WEDNESDAY 31

Be flexible

GOALS

FOR FEBRUARY

Things I want to accomplish

_____

Results I intend to achieve

_____

Gifts I want to buy

_____

Movies I want to see

Happiness is not something ready made. It comes from your own actions.

Dalai Lama

Until thought is linked with purpose there is no intelligent accomplishment.

Inez Bracy

FEBRUARY

Out on the edge you see all kinds of things you can't see from the centre. Big, undreamed-of things, the people on the edge see them first.

Kurt Vonnegut

Love isn't a state of perfect caring. It is an active noun like struggle. To love someone is to strive to accept that person exactly the way he or she is, right here and now.

Fred Rogers

Just because something doesn't do what you planned it to do, doesn't mean it's useless.

Thomas Edison

If it keeps up, man will atrophy all his limbs but the push-button finger.

Frank Lloyd Wright

THURSDAY 1

Don't stand in your own way

Remember, happiness doesn't depend upon who you are or what you have; it depends solely on what you think.

Dale Carnegie

I am convinced all of humanity is born with more gifts than we know. Most are born geniuses and just get de-geniused rapidly.

R Buckminster Fuller

Teamwork makes the dream work.

John C Maxwell

FRIDAY 2

Start your day with a to-do list

SATURDAY 3

Get excited about your plans

SUNDAY 4

Go where the door is open

19

FEBRUARY

THE FOUR AGREEMENTS

1. Be impeccable with your word

Speak with integrity. Say only what you mean. Avoid using your word to speak against yourself or to gossip about others. Use the power of your word in the direction of truth and love.

2. Don't take anything personally

Nothing others do is because of you. What others say and do is a projection of their own reality, their own dream. When you are immune to the opinions and actions of others, you won't be the victim of needless suffering.

3. Don't make assumptions

Find the courage to ask questions and to express what you really want. Communicate with others as clearly as you can to avoid misunderstandings, sadness and drama. With just this one agreement, you can completely transform your life.

4. Always do your best

Your best is going to change from moment to moment; it will be different when you are healthy as opposed to sick. Simply do your best under any circumstance to avoid self-judgment, self-abuse, and regret.

Miguel Ruiz

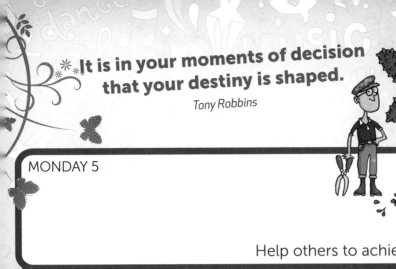

It is in your moments of decision that your destiny is shaped.

Tony Robbins

MONDAY 5

Help others to achieve their goals

TUESDAY 6

Notice what's happening around you

WEDNESDAY 7

Care enough to speak the truth

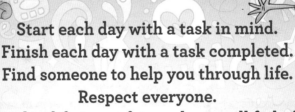

Start each day with a task in mind.
Finish each day with a task completed.
Find someone to help you through life.
Respect everyone.
Know that life is not fair and you will fail often.
Take some risks, step up when times are tough, face down
the bullies, lift up the downtrodden and don't give up.
Your job is to make this world a little
better than you found it.

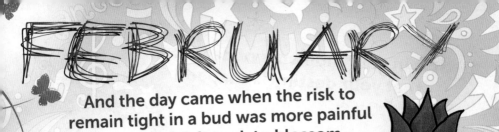

FEBRUARY

And the day came when the risk to remain tight in a bud was more painful than the risk it took to blossom.

Anais Nin

THURSDAY 8

If you have something to say, say it

FRIDAY 9

There are (at least) two sides to every story

SATURDAY 10

Things are not always as they seem

SUNDAY 11

Accept people as they are, and as they are not

You can become blind by seeing each day as a similar one. Each day is a different one, each day brings a miracle of its own. It's just a matter of paying attention to the miracle.

MONDAY 12

Remember you always have a choice

Life isn't about finding yourself, you are not lost. Look around. You are exactly where you are. Wherever you want to go, to get there, you must go from here. Don't be afraid to ask directions.

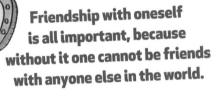

Friendship with oneself is all important, because without it one cannot be friends with anyone else in the world.

Eleanor Roosevelt

TUESDAY 13

Don't worry about the future – do something about it

WEDNESDAY 14   ST VALENTINE'S DAY

Tell your parents you love them

THURSDAY 15

Today is the first day of the rest of your life

FEBRUARY

Balance yourself. Accept yourself. Love yourself. Realise that life is beautiful because you are beautiful.

Kind words can be short and easy to speak, but their echoes are truly endless.

Mother Theresa

FRIDAY 16

Plan to achieve your full potential

SATURDAY 17

Don't sell out on anyone, especially yourself

SUNDAY 18

The last minute, unfortunately, has only 60 seconds

If you don't take any risks, reward is nearly impossible. If you take many risks, failure is always possible. If the reward is worth the risk, even if you fail, you will not have failed to try.

When life puts you in tough situations, don't say "why me?" say "try me".

MONDAY 19

Sing out loud wherever you can

TUESDAY 20

Learn to enjoy the merry-go-round

WEDNESDAY 21

Celebrate the achievements of others as well as your own

THURSDAY 22

You are only limited by your own thinking

*The future lies before you
Like a field of fallen snow,
Be careful how you tread on it
For every step will show.*

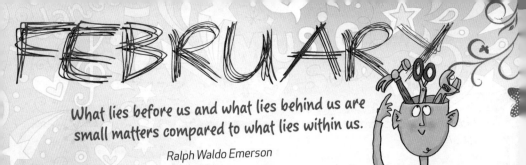

FEBRUARY

What lies before us and what lies behind us are small matters compared to what lies within us.

Ralph Waldo Emerson

FRIDAY 23

Don't put yourself in danger

SATURDAY 24

Never let your burdens paralyse your progress

SUNDAY 25

Temporary loss often results in permanent gain

Unless your heart, your soul, and your whole being are behind every decision you make, the words from your mouth will be empty, and each action meaningless. Truth and confidence are the roots of happiness.

Pietro Aretino

Feeling sorry for yourself, and your present condition, is not only a waste of energy, it's the worst habit you could possibly have.

TRUTH

I'm a big believer that when you choose happiness, then success will follow. Happiness encourages good life decisions, bolsters wonderful relationships, and opens up doors to great opportunities.

I bargained with Life for a penny,
And Life would pay no more,
However I begged at evening
When I counted my scanty store;

For Life is a just employer,
He gives you what you ask,
But once you have set the wages,
Why, you must bear the task.

I worked for a menial's hire,
Only to learn, dismayed,
That any wage I had asked of Life,
Life would have paid.

Jessie Belle Rittenhouse

MONDAY 26

Remember why your friends are your friends

TUESDAY 27

Embrace what others love about you

WEDNESDAY 28

Goals are dreams with deadlines

GOALS

FOR MARCH

The safest investment to make is in your future. Read at least 30 minutes a day, listen to relevant podcasts and seek out mentors. Consume knowledge like air and put your pursuit of learning above all else.

The difficulty lies not so much in developing new ideas as in escaping from old ones.

John Maynard Keynes

Things I want to accomplish

Results I intend to achieve

Books I want to read

Competitions I want to enter

My dreams

Allow your mind to wander – it goes places where ideas happen.

Here's to the crazy ones. The misfits. The rebels. The troublemakers. The round pegs in the square holes. The ones who see things differently. They're not fond of rules. And they have no respect for the status quo. You can quote them, disagree with them, glorify or vilify them. But the only thing you can't do is ignore them. Because they change things. They push the human race forward. And while some may see them as the crazy ones, we see genius. Because the people who are crazy enough to think they can change the world, are the ones who do.

Rob Siltanen

THURSDAY 1

This too will pass

FRIDAY 2

Worry about it tomorrow

SATURDAY 3

Challenge your own limits

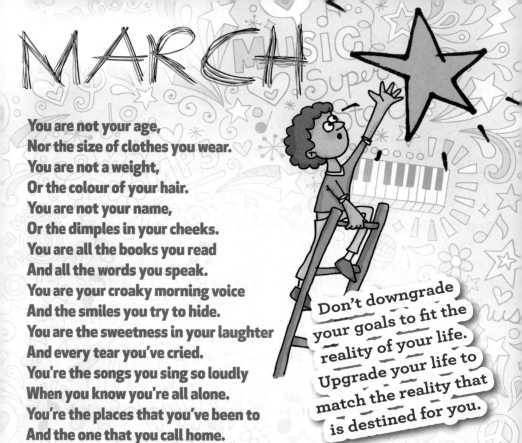

You are not your age,
Nor the size of clothes you wear.
You are not a weight,
Or the colour of your hair.
You are not your name,
Or the dimples in your cheeks.
You are all the books you read
And all the words you speak.
You are your croaky morning voice
And the smiles you try to hide.
You are the sweetness in your laughter
And every tear you've cried.
You're the songs you sing so loudly
When you know you're all alone.
You're the places that you've been to
And the one that you call home.
You're the things that you believe in
And the people that you love.
You're the photos in your bedroom
And the future you dream of.
You're made of so much beauty
And it seems that you forgot.
When you decided that you were defined
By all the things you're not.

Ernest Hemingway

Don't downgrade your goals to fit the reality of your life. Upgrade your life to match the reality that is destined for you.

SUNDAY 4

Notice the unusual

30

> *People are like stained glass windows. They sparkle and shine when the sun is out, but when the darkness sets in, their true beauty is revealed only if there is a light from within*
>
> Elisabeth Kubler Ross

MONDAY 5

Actions speak louder than words

> *There is nothing in a caterpillar that tells you it's going to be a butterfly.*
>
> R Buckminster Fuller

TUESDAY 6

Honesty is always the best policy

WEDNESDAY 7

Bravery is always rewarded

THURSDAY 8

No one can keep you down but yourself

MARCH

RISKS

To laugh is to risk appearing the fool. To weep is to risk appearing sentimental. To reach out for another is to risk involvement. To expose feelings is to risk exposing your true self. To place your ideas, your dreams, before a crowd is to risk their loss. To love is to risk being loved in return. To live is to risk dying. To hope is to risk despair. To try is to risk failure. But risks must be taken, because the greatest hazard in life is to risk nothing. The person who risks nothing, does nothing, has nothing, and is nothing. They may avoid suffering and sorrow, but they cannot learn, feel, change, grow, love or live. Chained by their attitudes, they are slaves, They have forfeited their freedom. Only a person who risks is free.

William Arthur Ward

FRIDAY 9

Every job is as hard or easy as the imagination makes it

SATURDAY 10

In every conflict there is growth

SUNDAY 11 MOTHER'S DAY

Don't expect something for nothing

Learn as much as you can about as much as you can

Friends are angels who lift our feet when our own wings have trouble remembering how to fly.

ODDS

Success has no address, no landmark, no calling card. But the path is steep, and some will take the elevator, but I will take the stairs. Some will get there faster, but I will get there stronger. And adversity will be my travelling companion. because when I get there, I can turn to adversity and say, so long. And heave the bag of taunts that I gathered along the way and scatter them to the birds. I will miss them, but I wll feel lighter. Yes, that will be the day, when I stand by a window and unclench my fists. For there will be no more odds to conquer, not even in the mind. I like odds, they help me get even!

TUESDAY 13

Life is a voyage of discovery

MARCH

Keep away from people who try to belittle your ambitions.

WEDNESDAY 14

Everyone smiles in the same language

THURSDAY 15

Be kind, everyone is dealing with something

Talent hits a target no one else can hit.
Genius hits a target no one else can see.

If you think you are too small to make a difference, you have never spent the night with a mosquito.

FRIDAY 16

Go slowly in the direction of your dreams

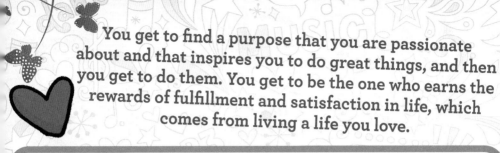

You get to find a purpose that you are passionate about and that inspires you to do great things, and then you get to do them. You get to be the one who earns the rewards of fulfillment and satisfaction in life, which comes from living a life you love.

SATURDAY 17

Happy 🍀 St. Patricks Day

SUNDAY 18

Reflect on your experiences

SIX BEST DOCTORS IN THE WORLD:

1. Sunlight
2. Rest
3. Exercise
4. Food
5. Friends
6. Fun

For attractive lips, speak words of kindness. **For lovely eyes,** seek out the good in people. **For a slim figure,** share your food with the hungry. **For beautiful hair,** let a child run their fingers through it once a day. **For poise,** walk with the knowledge you'll never walk alone.

Remember, if you ever need **a helping hand,** you'll find one at the end of your arm. As you grow older, you will discover that you have **two hands:** one for helping yourself, the other for **helping others.**

There will be a new voice which you will slowly recognise as your own, that will keep you company as you stride deeper and deeper into the world.

Mary Oliver

MARCH

Happy people are beautiful.
They become like a mirror and they
reflect that happiness.

Drew Barrymore

MONDAY 19 **BANK HOLIDAY**

Some things you just cannot control

TUESDAY 20

Your health is your most treasured possession

WEDNESDAY 21

There are no stupid questions

THURSDAY 22

Share your heart and follow where it leads

FRIDAY 23

Finish the day with a 'done list'

THE POWER OF ONE ...

One song can spark a moment,
One flower can wake the dream,
One tree can start a forest,
One bird can herald spring
One smile begins a friendship,
One handclasp lifts a soul,
One star can guide a ship at sea,
One word can frame the goal,
One vote can change a nation,
One sunbeam lights a room,
One candle wipes out darkness,
One laugh will conquer gloom,
One step must start each journey,
One word must start each prayer,
One hope will raise your spirits,
One touch can show you care,
One voice can speak with wisdom,
One heart can know what's true,
One life can make the difference,
You see, it's up to you.

You are the only person you can actually change.

You have within you the ability to accomplish almost anything you set your mind to, whether it's learning a new skill, kicking a bad habit, or fulfilling your own life's dream.

We either make ourselves miserable or we make ourselves strong, the amount of work required is the same.

MARCH

SATURDAY 24

Don't waste your energy on revenge or regret

This life is what you make it. No matter what, you're going to mess up sometimes, it's a universal truth. But the good part is you get to decide how you're going to mess it up. Girls will be your friends – they'll act like it anyway. But just remember, some come, some go. The ones that stay with you through everything – they're your true best friends. Don't let go of them. Also remember, sisters make the best friends in the world. As for lovers, well, they'll come and go too. And baby, I hate to say it, most of them – actually pretty much all of them are going to break your heart, but you can't give up because if you give up, you'll never find your soulmate. You'll never find that half who makes you whole and that goes for everything. Just because you fail once, doesn't mean you're gonna fail at everything. Keep trying, hold on, and always, always, always believe in yourself, because if you don't, then who will, sweetie? So keep your head high, keep your chin up, and most importantly, keep smiling, because life's a beautiful thing and there's so much to smile about.

Marilyn Monroe

SUNDAY 25

Be a loyal friend

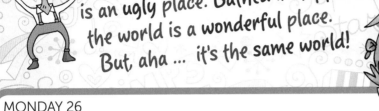
Consumed with anger, the world is an ugly place. Bathed in happiness, the world is a wonderful place. But, aha ... it's the same world!

MONDAY 26

Confidence grows slowly

TUESDAY 27

Decide who you want to be in the world – and go be that

WEDNESDAY 28

Don't forget, even for one day, how special you are

THURSDAY 29

It's an 'us' world

FRIDAY 30 GOOD FRIDAY

You will recover from heartache

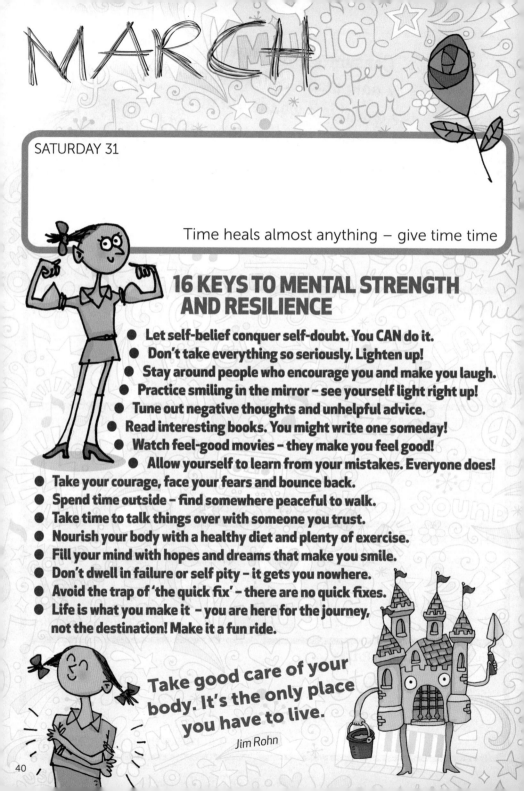

MARCH

Time heals almost anything – give time time

16 KEYS TO MENTAL STRENGTH AND RESILIENCE

- Let self-belief conquer self-doubt. You CAN do it.
- Don't take everything so seriously. Lighten up!
- Stay around people who encourage you and make you laugh.
- Practice smiling in the mirror – see yourself light right up!
- Tune out negative thoughts and unhelpful advice.
- Read interesting books. You might write one someday!
- Watch feel-good movies – they make you feel good!
- Allow yourself to learn from your mistakes. Everyone does!
- Take your courage, face your fears and bounce back.
- Spend time outside – find somewhere peaceful to walk.
- Take time to talk things over with someone you trust.
- Nourish your body with a healthy diet and plenty of exercise.
- Fill your mind with hopes and dreams that make you smile.
- Don't dwell in failure or self pity – it gets you nowhere.
- Avoid the trap of 'the quick fix' – there are no quick fixes.
- Life is what you make it – you are here for the journey, not the destination! Make it a fun ride.

Take good care of your body. It's the only place you have to live.

Jim Rohn

GOALS FOR APRIL

I want you to talk to yourself. Nicely. Imagine someone who loves you saying the kind words you want to hear. Now say them to yourself.

Things I want to accomplish

Results I intend to achieve

Talents I want to practice

Sports I want to try

Let the beauty we love be what we do.
Rumi

SUNDAY 1 **EASTER SUNDAY**

Every down side has an upside

41

APRIL

If you want to go fast, go alone.
If you want to go far, go together.

African proverb

He who angers you, controls you.
Whatever is begun in anger,
ends in shame.

Benjamin Franklin

MONDAY 2 BANK HOLIDAY

It's important to have fun

TUESDAY 3

Dance lightly with life

WEDNESDAY 4

Not all stress is bad

*I do think something very magical
can happen when you read a good book.*

JK Rowling

**I learned many years ago that the future has
nothing planned for me. I must plan my future.
By the way, it's the same for you.**

THURSDAY 5

Spend time listening to others

FRIDAY 6

Be grateful for what you have

Can you remember who you were, before the world told you who you should be?

Charles Bukowski

It is literally true that you can succeed best and quickest by helping others to succeed.

Napoleon Hill

SATURDAY 7

Your reputation is always left behind you

SUNDAY 8

When you mess up, fess up

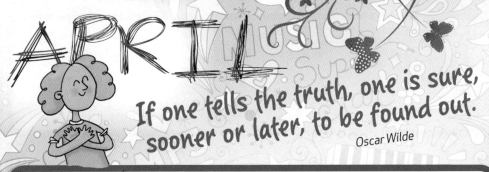

APRIL

If one tells the truth, one is sure, sooner or later, to be found out.

Oscar Wilde

MONDAY 9

Don't let your parents down; they brought you up

TUESDAY 10

Your phone will not hug you when you are sad

WEDNESDAY 11

Smile in the mirror at least once per day

THURSDAY 12

It's a sad day that has no smile

FRIDAY 13

There will always be a choice

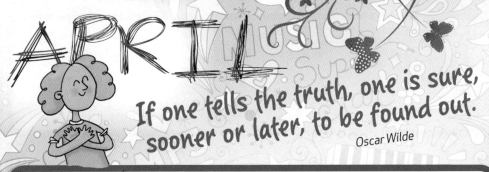

Kids are often asked: *'What do you want to BE when you grow up?'* The world expects grandiose aspirations: *'I want to be a writer, a doctor, the prime minister.'* They're told: go to school, go to college, get a job, get married, and then you'll be happy.

But that's all about doing, not being – and while doing will bring you moments of joy, it won't necessarily reward you with lasting happiness.

Stop and breathe. BE healthy. BE friendly. BE interested. BE around your friends and family. BE there for someone, and let someone be there for you. BE courageous. BE generous. BE honest. BE loyal. BE bold. Just BE for a minute.

If you allow yourself to be in the moment, in the here and now, and appreciate the moment, happiness will show up where you are. There's a reason we're called human **BE**ings and not human doings. As human beings we have the ability to think, move and communicate in a unique way. We can cooperate, understand, reconcile and love, that's what sets us apart from most other species.

Don't waste your human talents by stressing about small things, for that which you cannot change. If you take the time simply to be grateful for the good things in your life, your stresses will begin to dissolve, and you will be happier. But don't just seek happiness when you're down. Happiness shouldn't be a goal, it should be a habit. Take the focus off doing, and start being every day.

BE loving, **BE** grateful, **BE** helpful.

Allow yourself to be in the moment, and appreciate the moment. Take the focus off everything you think you need to do, and start being. I promise you, happiness will follow.

Richard Branson

SATURDAY 14

Read travel stories to broaden your mind

SUNDAY 15

The world is an amazing place waiting to be explored

APRIL

There is no right way to do the wrong thing.

MONDAY 16

Yes, you can change the world ... but it takes time!

TUESDAY 17

In your heart you know

WEDNESDAY 18

You don't need to always follow the crowd

THURSDAY 19

You will never regret doing your best

Everyone has inside of them a piece of good news.
The good news is that you don't know how great
you can be! How much you can love!
What you can accomplish!
And what your potential is!

Anne Frank

Few things in the world are more powerful than a positive push. A smile. A world of optimism and hope. A 'you can do it' attitude when things are tough.

FRIDAY 20

Kind communication is the key to happy relationships

SATURDAY 21

Listen, listen, listen ...

SUNDAY 22

Invest time in growing your friendships

You wouldn't worry so much about what others think of you if you realised how seldom they do.

Eleanor Roosevelt

Everyone wants to live on top of the mountain, but all the happiness and growth occurs while you're climbing it.

Andy Rooney

Anger blows out the lamp of the mind.

Robert Ingersoll

APRIL

MONDAY 23

Have fun doing what you're doing

People are lonely because they build walls instead of bridges.

Make the most of yourself — for that is all there is of you.
Ralph Waldo Emerson

Above all else, never think you are not enough.

TUESDAY 24

Learn the joy of giving

WEDNESDAY 25

Never give up on what's important

THURSDAY 26

Allow yourself to wonder

HOW TO BE MORE CONFIDENT

Don't compare yourself with others. It is OK to do it your way.
Be prepared and always plan on giving your best.
Dress up. When you look good, you feel good.
Relax. Cool goes well with confidence.
Trust yourself. You are more capable than you think.
Ignore your inner critic – it lies!
Keep a positive attitude – optimism is always confident.
Smile and enjoy the occasion.
Be interested in others, they may be less confident than you.
Love what you do – it always shows.

Education is the most powerful weapon that you can use to change the world.
Nelson Mandela

Sticks, in a bundle, are unbreakable.
Kenyan proverb

FRIDAY 27

Reach out to others – make the first step

SATURDAY 28

Develop your strength in small matters

SUNDAY 29

Read a good book, any good book

MONDAY 30

When you lose don't lose the lesson

You have a gift, talent, or perspective in life that no one else has, and your purpose is to share that with the world. Whether you have a gift of speaking, writing, singing, or simply caring for others, your true purpose is to be you and share those gifts with the people around you. Life is too precious to leave your song unsung, your book unwritten, or your dreams undone. Stop questioning if you are good enough, special enough, or gifted enough to do it. You absolutely are!

I think, at a child's birth, if a mother could ask a fairy godmother to endow it with the most useful gift, that gift would be curiosity.

Eleanor Roosevelt

GOALS FOR MAY

Things I want to accomplish

Results I intend to achieve

Sports I want to try

Amount I want to save

Continuous effort, not strength or intelligence, is the key to unlocking your full potential.
Winston Churchill

The heaviest load to carry is a bundle of grudges.

MAX

It has become appallingly obvious that our technology has exceeded our humanity.

Albert Einstein

Of the things you say, and think and do,
Ask yourself "Is it true?"
"Is it right and is it fair?"
"Is it the kind of thing to share?"
Will it make the world a better place?
Or simply make me a disgrace?
What I do is up to me,
But it's there for everyone to see.

There is nothing wrong with having a bad day. There is everything wrong with making others have to have it with you.

Neil Cavuto

TUESDAY 1

Share the burden

WEDNESDAY 2

Go easy on yourself and go easy on others

THURSDAY 3

Listen to understand

> *Once you replace negative thoughts with positive ones, you'll start having positive results.*
>
> Willie Nelson

FRIDAY 4

Tidy up your own mess

SATURDAY 5

Do what you enjoy

SUNDAY 6

For a straight answer, ask a straight question

Our deepest fear is not that we are inadequate. Our deepest fear is that we are powerful beyond measure. It is our light, not our darkness that most frightens us. We ask ourselves, "Who am I to be brilliant, gorgeous, talented, fabulous?" Actually, who are you not to be? You are a child of God. Your playing small does not serve the world. There is nothing enlightened about shrinking so that other people won't feel insecure around you. We are all meant to shine, as children do. We were born to make manifest the glory of God that is within us. It's not just in some of us; it's in everyone. And as we let our own light shine, we unconsciously give other people permission to do the same. As we are liberated from our own fear, our presence automatically liberates others.

Marianne Williamson

MAY

'What is REAL?' asked the Rabbit one day, when they were lying side by side near the nursery fender, before Nana came to tidy the room. 'Does it mean having things that buzz inside you and a stick-out handle?'

'Real isn't how you are made,' said the Skin Horse. 'It's a thing that happens to you. When a child loves you for a long, long time, not just to play with, but REALLY loves you, then you become Real.'

'Does it hurt?' asked the Rabbit.

'Sometimes,' said the Skin Horse, for he was always truthful. 'When you are Real you don't mind being hurt.'

'Does it happen all at once, like being wound up,' he asked, 'or bit by bit?'

'It doesn't happen all at once,' said the Skin Horse. 'You become. It takes a long time. That's why it doesn't happen often to those who break easily, or have sharp edges, or who have to be carefully kept. Generally, by the time you are Real, most of your hair has been loved off, and your eyes drop out and you get loose in the joints and very shabby. But these things don't matter at all, because once you are Real you can't be ugly, except to people who don't understand.'

Margery Williams (The Velveteen Rabbit)

MONDAY 7 **BANK HOLIDAY**

You get from people what you expect

54

Life is more interesting when you say yes!

Richard Branson

TUESDAY 8

Decide what you want and go for it

WEDNESDAY 9

Finish what you start

THURSDAY 10

Chose your companions with care

FRIDAY 11

For true happiness, have no enemies

Hiking is a bit like life. The journey only requires you to put one foot in front of the other – again and again and again. And if you allow yourself the opportunity to be present throughout the entirety of the trek, you will witness beauty every step on the way, not just at the summit.

MAY

Two monologues do not make a dialogue.

Jeff Daly

SATURDAY 12

Be someone who makes a positive difference

SUNDAY 13

Say 'Thank You' a lot

Do not let your fire go out, spark by irreplaceable spark in the hopeless swamps of the not-quite, the not-yet, and the not-at-all. Do not let the hero in your soul perish in lonely frustration for the life you deserved and have never been able to reach. The world you desire can be won. It exists... it is real... it is possible... it's yours.

Ayn Rand

TOP 10 THINGS TO THINK ABOUT IF YOU WANT TO CHANGE THE WORLD

1) All significant change happens as the result of the courage and commitment of individuals.
2) Believe that you have a unique purpose and potential in the world.
3) You can choose the difference you want to make.
4) The world may be big but there are no small things – everyone and everything matters.
5) If you want to see change in the world you have to BE the change you want to see.
6) Find a team where your talents are strengths.
7) Don't wait for things to be right to begin. Start where you are.
8) Take to heart the words of Albert Einstein: "All meaningful and lasting change starts first in your imagination and then works its way out. Imagination is more important than knowledge."
9) In order for things in your life to change, YOU have to change something.
10) We can't change others, we can only change ourselves. When we change, everything changes. If there is something you don't like about your life, or the world, change it or change the way you think about it.

When you change the way you look at things, the things you look at change.

% Chances of success

I WON'T – 0%
I CAN'T – 10%
I DON'T KNOW HOW – 20%
I WISH I COULD – 30%
I WANT TO – 40%
I THINK I MIGHT – 50%
I THINK I CAN – 60%
I THINK I WILL – 70%
I KNOW I CAN – 80%
I KNOW I WILL – 90%
I DID – 100%

MAY

One of the most beautiful gifts in the world is the gift of encouragement. When someone encourages you, that person helps you over a threshold you might otherwise never have crossed on your own.

John O'Donohue

MONDAY 14

Avoid jumping to conclusions

TUESDAY 15

Take care of yourself

WEDNESDAY 16

You can only swim when you learn to trust the water

THURSDAY 17

We are all perfectly imperfect

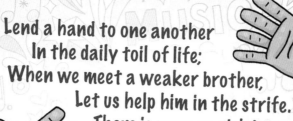

Lend a hand to one another
In the daily toil of life;
When we meet a weaker brother,
Let us help him in the strife.
There is none so rich but may,
In his turn, be forced to borrow;
And the poor man's lot to-day
May become our own to-morrow.

FRIDAY 18

Give your body the nourishment it deserves

SATURDAY 19

Be your own best friend first

SUNDAY 20

Don't exaggerate the negatives

When I was five years old, my mother always told me that happiness was the key to life. When I went to school, they asked me what I wanted to be when I grew up. I wrote down 'happy'. They told me I didn't understand the assignment, and I told them they didn't understand life.

John Lennon

Everyone should be able to do one card trick, tell two jokes, and recite three poems, in case they are ever trapped in an elevator.

The two kinds of people

There are two kinds of people on earth to-day;
Just two kinds of people, no more, I say.
Not the sinner and saint, for it's well understood,
The good are half bad and the bad are half good.
Not the rich and the poor, for to rate a man's wealth,
You must first know the state of his conscience and health.
No; the two kinds of people on earth I mean,
Are the people who lift and the people who lean.

Ella Wheeler Wilcox

MONDAY 21

We are all ordinary, and we can all be extraordinary

TUESDAY 22

The world needs your unique contribution

WEDNESDAY 23

The future hasn't happened yet – you can influence it

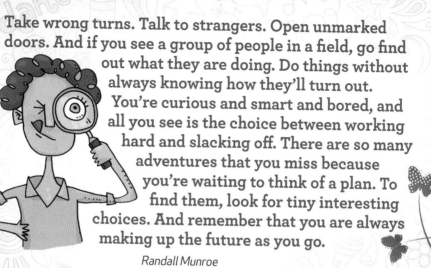

Take wrong turns. Talk to strangers. Open unmarked doors. And if you see a group of people in a field, go find out what they are doing. Do things without always knowing how they'll turn out. You're curious and smart and bored, and all you see is the choice between working hard and slacking off. There are so many adventures that you miss because you're waiting to think of a plan. To find them, look for tiny interesting choices. And remember that you are always making up the future as you go.

Randall Munroe

THURSDAY 24

Trust you are in the perfect place

FRIDAY 25

Don't suffer with silent secrets

SATURDAY 26

Sometimes, it's ok to let go

SUNDAY 27

Balance your negative thoughts with positive ones

MAX

Strength does not come from winning. Your struggles develop your strengths. When you go through hardships and choose not to surrender, that is strength.

MONDAY 28

Shine your light

TUESDAY 29

Be trustworthy

WEDNESDAY 30

Take up playing a musical instrument

THURSDAY 31

Enjoy the beauty of a garden

GOALS

FOR JUNE

You have brains in your head, feet in your shoes, You can steer yourself in any direction you choose.
Dr Seuss

Things I want to accomplish

Results I intend to achieve

Games I want to play

Places I want to visit

My dreams

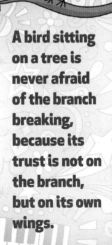

A bird sitting on a tree is never afraid of the branch breaking, because its trust is not on the branch, but on its own wings.

JUNE

WHY GOD MADE TEACHERS

When God created teachers,
He gave us special friends
To help us understand this world
And truly comprehend
The beauty and the wonder
Of everything we see,
And become a better person
With each discovery.
When God created teachers,
He gave us special guides
To show us ways in which to grow
So we can all decide
How to live and how to do
What's right instead of wrong,
To lead us so that we can lead
And learn how to be strong.
Why God created teachers
In his wisdom and his grace
Was to help us learn to make our world
A better, wiser place.

She worked by day
And toiled by night.
She gave up play
And some delight.
Dry books she read,
New things to learn.
And forged ahead,
Success to earn.
She plodded on
With faith and pluck.
And when she won,
They called it luck!

And those who were seen dancing were thought to be insane by those who could not hear the music.

Friedrich Nietzsche

FRIDAY 1

Nurture your friendships with care

64

PROMISE YOURSELF

To be so strong that nothing
Can disturb your peace of mind.
To talk health, happiness, and prosperity
To every person you meet.

To make all your friends feel
That there is something worthwhile in them
To look at the sunny side of everything
And make your optimism come true.

To think only of the best, to work only for the best,
And to expect only the best.
To be just as enthusiastic about the success of others
As you are about your own.

To forget the mistakes of the past
And press on to the greater achievements of the future.
To wear a cheerful expression at all times
And give a smile to every living creature you meet.

To give so much time to improving yourself
That you have no time to criticise others.
To be too large for worry, too noble for anger,
too strong for fear,
And too happy to permit the presence of trouble.

To think well of yourself and to proclaim this fact to the world,
Not in loud words but great deeds.
To live the faith that the whole world is on your side
So long as you are true to the best that is in you.

Christian D Larson

65

JUNE

And forget not that the earth delights to feel your bare feet and the winds long to play with your hair.

Kahlil Gibran

SATURDAY 2

Do ordinary things in an extraordinary way

SUNDAY 3

Never speak badly, even to yourself

There is no "perfect" time to do anything. Do yourself a favour and stop waiting for the perfect time. The time the opportunity presents is the perfect time to take advantage of that opportunity.

People do not seem to realise that their opinion of the world is also a confession of their character.

Ralph Waldo Emerson

Do what you can, with what you have, where you are.
Theodore Roosevelt

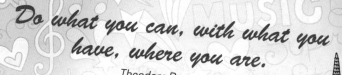

A rock pile ceases to be a rock pile the moment a single man contemplates it, bearing within him the image of a cathedral
Antoine de Saint-Exupéry

MONDAY 4 BANK HOLIDAY

A little love goes a long way

TUESDAY 5

The future is as bright as you are prepared to make it

WEDNESDAY 6

Your intuition is powerful; listen to it

THURSDAY 7

Where there's a will there's a way

JUNE

Your attitude is like a *box of crayons* that colour your world.
Constantly colour your picture grey, and your picture will always be bleak.
Try adding some bright colours to the picture by including humour, and your picture begins to brighten up.

FRIDAY 8

Plan your career around your talents

SATURDAY 9

Browse in a good bookshop

SUNDAY 10

Spend time chatting with friends

Individually we may be one drop, but together we can make up an ocean.

Things turn out best for those who make the best out of the way things turn out.

MONDAY 11

Write things down

TUESDAY 12

Have a tech free day

WEDNESDAY 13

Learn from your mistakes

THURSDAY 14

It takes courage to tell the truth

FRIDAY 15

Most of what you worry about never happens

JUNE

SATURDAY 16

Stay connected to your friends and family

SUNDAY 17 FATHER'S DAY

Never hesitate to say 'I'm sorry'

And once this storm is over, you won't remember how you made it through, how you managed to survive. You won't even be sure whether the storm is really over. But one thing is certain. When you come out of the storm, you won't be the same person who went in. That's what this storm's all about.

Stepping outside your comfort zone is difficult, but courage gives you the mental strength to face your fears head on.

Inaction may be the highest form of action.

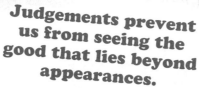

Judgements prevent us from seeing the good that lies beyond appearances.

Wayne Dyer

Be content with what you have, rejoice in the way things are. When you realise there is nothing lacking, the whole world belongs to you.

Lao Tzu

MONDAY 18

We all dance to the beat of a different drum

TUESDAY 19

We can all feel lonely at times

WEDNESDAY 20

Jealousy is a dangerous emotion

THURSDAY 21

Stay awake to the real world

JUNE

Whether you think you can, or you think you can't – you're right.

Henry Ford

Everyone is a genius, but if you judge a fish on its ability to climb a tree it will spend its whole life believing it is stupid.

Albert Einstein

The flower that blooms in adversity is the rarest and most beautiful of all.

Walt Disney

FRIDAY 22

Pay attention to your education

SATURDAY 23

Work will be rewarded

SUNDAY 24

Learn the art of conversation

Sometimes, to be what you want to be, you must give up being what you are.

Almost everything you do will seem insignificant, but it is important that you do it.
Mahatma Gandhi

Try not to become a person of success. Rather become a person of value.
Albert Einstein

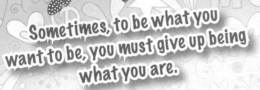

MONDAY 25

Develop a forgiving attitude

TUESDAY 26

Life is not always fair but it always turns out fine

WEDNESDAY 27

You have all your life in front of you

JUNE

A life spent making mistakes is not only more honorable, but more useful than a life spent doing nothing.

George Bernard Shaw

THURSDAY 28

Stay away from anything that dulls your mind

FRIDAY 29

In the game of life, be a good sport

SATURDAY 30

Learn to surf the waves of life

In the end, we will remember not the words of our enemies, but the silence of our friends.

Martin Luther King JR

You have enemies? Good. That means you've stood up for something, sometime in your life.

Winston Churchill

GOALS

FOR JULY

Things I want to accomplish

_____

Results I intend to achieve

_____

Places I want to visit

_____

Games I want to play

Hope is the thing with feathers
That perches in the soul
And sings the tune without the words
And never stops at all.

Emily Dickinson

JULY

WORDS

DID is a word of achievement.
WON'T is a word of retreat.
MIGHT is a word of bereavement.
CAN'T is a word of defeat.
OUGHT is a word of duty.
TRY is a word each hour.
CAN is a word of beauty.
WILL is a word of power.

NOTICE TO TEENAGERS

If you're being hassled by your parents, move out and make your own way in the world. While you still know everything.

The most powerful nation on earth is your imagination.

SUNDAY 1

Get out into nature

Don't take it personally. What others say and do is a projection of their own reality. When you are immune to the opinions and actions of others, you won't be the victim of needless suffering.

Your words are powerful. Your words can create the most beautiful dream, or your words can destroy everything around you. Be mindful of your words.

DO IT ANYWAY

People are often unreasonable, illogical and self centered; Forgive them anyway. If you are kind, people may accuse you of selfish, ulterior motives; Be kind anyway. If you are successful, you will win some false friends and some true enemies; Succeed anyway. If you are honest and frank, people may cheat you; Be honest and frank anyway. What you spend years building, someone could destroy overnight; Build anyway. If you find serenity and happiness, they may be jealous; Be happy anyway. The good you do today, people will often forget tomorrow; Do good anyway. Give the world the best you have, and it may never be enough; Give the world the best you've got anyway. You see, in the final analysis, it is between you and God; It was never between you and them anyway.

Mother Teresa

Be who you are and say what you feel, because those who mind don't matter, and those who matter don't mind.

Be yourself, everyone else is already taken.

Oscar Wilde

77

JULY

What's in a name? That which we call a rose, by any other name, would smell as sweet.

William Shakespeare

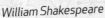

MONDAY 2

Change happens to us all

TUESDAY 3

Opportunity often knocks very softly

WEDNESDAY 4

Trust in yourself and all that you are

THURSDAY 5

You are good enough and there's always room for improvement

FRIDAY 6

Happiness is an inside job

Nobody has ever measured, not even poets, how much love the heart can hold.

Zelda Fitzgerald

SATURDAY 7

Don't suffer in silence – speak to someone you trust

SUNDAY 8

Spend time with older people

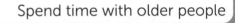

I wanted a perfect ending. Now I've learned, the hard way, that some poems don't rhyme, and some stories don't have a clear beginning, middle, and end. Life is about not knowing, having to change, taking the moment and making the best of it, without knowing what's going to happen next.

Gilda Radner

If I had a flower for every time I thought of you ... I could walk through my garden forever.

Alfred Tennyson

JULY

Above all, be the hero of your own life, not the victim.

HERO

MONDAY 9

Go with the flow or swim against the tide

TUESDAY 10

People are really interesting when you get to know them

WEDNESDAY 11

Everything you are for, strengthens you

It is one of the most beautiful compensations of life, that no one can sincerely try to help another without helping himself.
Ralph Waldo Emerson

For good mental health keep your heart cheerful and your mind optimistic, hopeful and always willing to discover something new.

Life is an ever flowing process, and somewhere on the river of life, unpleasant things will pop up – they may even leave a scar – but then life is flowing, and like experience, teaches us a lesson. Keep swimming with the current, because life is such that sometimes it is nice and sometimes it is not.

THURSDAY 12

Think of all the possibilities that lie ahead

FRIDAY 13

Life is a slowly unfolding process – be patient

SATURDAY 14

There is no shortcut to greatness

SUNDAY 15

Necessity is the mother of invention

JULY

A lot of problems in the world would disappear by people talking to each other instead of talking about each other.

We should all be thankful for those people who rekindle the inner spirit.

Albert Schweitzer

MONDAY 16

You become like the people you associate with

TUESDAY 17

Find an inspiring role model to show you the way

WEDNESDAY 18

Never be afraid to ask directions

THURSDAY 19

Accept offers of support

> *Fantasy is a necessary ingredient in living. It's a way of looking at life through the wrong end of a telescope.*
>
> Dr Seuss

FRIDAY 20

Be kind to your pet

SATURDAY 21

Everything you are against, weakens you

SUNDAY 22

You are more capable than you realise.

> **Your work is going to fill a large part of your life, and the only way to be truly satisfied is to do what you believe is great work. And the only way to do great work is to love what you do. If you haven't found it yet, keep looking. Don't settle. As with all matters of the heart, you'll know when you find it. And, like any great relationship, it just gets better and better as the years roll on. So keep looking until you find it. Don't settle.**
>
> Steve Jobs

JULY

And now that you don't have to be perfect, you can be good.

John Steinbeck

MONDAY 23

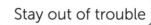

Stay out of trouble

Our greatest weakness lies in giving up. The most certain way to succeed is always to try just one more time.

Thomas A Edison

Life is like riding a bicycle. To keep your balance, you must keep moving.

Albert Einstein

TUESDAY 24

For all of us there are many turning points in our lives

Why fit in when you were born to stand out?
Dr Seuss

Positive anything is better than negative nothing.
Elbert Hubbard

WEDNESDAY 25

The cure for loneliness is in your heart

THURSDAY 26

Light a candle for someone who is unwell

FRIDAY 27

Spare a thought for those less fortunate

SATURDAY 28

Everyone has a place

SUNDAY 29

Don't get stuck on competing – look at collaborating

JULY

Write it on your heart that every day is the best day in the year. He is rich who owns the day, and no one owns the day who allows it to be invaded with fret and anxiety. This new day is too dear, with its hopes and invitations, to waste a moment on the yesterdays.

Ralph Waldo Emerson

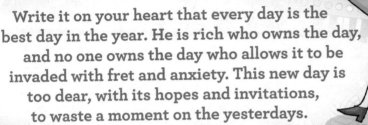

MONDAY 30

Life is better with a good giggle

TUESDAY 31

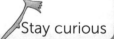

Stay curious

It is only in our darkest hours that we may discover the true strength of the brilliant light within ourselves that can never, ever, be dimmed.

Doe Zantamata

Dance like there's nobody watching,
Love like you'll never be hurt,
Sing like there's nobody listening,
And live like it's heaven on earth.

GOALS

FOR AUGUST

Things I want to accomplish

Results I intend to achieve

Competitions I want to enter

Movies I want to see

You may say I'm a dreamer, but I'm not the only one. I hope someday you'll join us, and the world will live as one.

John Lennon

WEDNESDAY 1

Don't be afraid to speak about what is important to you

AUGUST

*If you can dream it,
you can do it.
Always remember that this whole thing
was started with a dream
and a mouse.*

Walt Disney

THURSDAY 2

A pint of sweat saves a gallon of blood

FRIDAY 3

Ultimately, things don't matter, people do

SATURDAY 4

Forge your own path

SUNDAY 5

Aim high

Dear Daughter,

Here is my best advice for a beautiful life:

Never let anyone dull your flame. Do not let the world harden your heart. Love and take care of your body it is the only one you have. Nourish it so that it will fuel you for success. And remember, you are beautiful the way you are.

Believe in yourself. Follow your dreams and work to make those dreams come true. Laugh often, it warms the heart. Cry when you need to. Love as much as you can, it heals everything.

Think before you speak, and speak from your heart. What you say will be forgotten but the way you make someone feel will never be. Don't judge others. Everyone has their own struggles. If you judge them you can't love them.

Stand up for what is right. The greatest things are not always achieved by following the crowd but by leading it. Be brave and stand your own ground.

Always lend a helping hand. Never turn a blind eye to someone in need. Go out of your way to make someone smile. Doing good deeds will reap the greatest rewards. Take the time to discover and develop your own special talents and make a living doing what you love to do.

Keep your promises. Don't give your word if you are not going to honour it. Breaking someones trust is the hardest thing to rebuild.

See the world. Enjoy its beauty. Be kind to it, and do your bit to preserve it for others and future generations. Spread your wings, take the world head on. Be the strong, independent woman you were born to be and never feel alone in this world.

You will always be my daughter and you will always have a home in my heart.

Love Mom.

If you run into a wall, don't turn around and give up. Figure out how to climb it, go through it, or work around it.

Michael Jordan

AUGUST

What you do today can improve all your tomorrows.

Ralph Marston

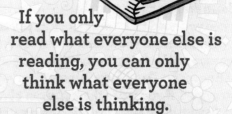

If you only read what everyone else is reading, you can only think what everyone else is thinking.

MONDAY 6 BANK HOLIDAY

Develop a habit of saving

TUESDAY 7

Don't make mischief

WEDNESDAY 8

Trust in the goodness of people

THURSDAY 9

Remain warm and approachable

> A group becomes a team when each member is sure enough of himself and his contribution to praise the skills of others.
>
> *Norman Shidle*

If you are still searching for that one person who will change your life, take a look in the mirror.

Never forget the fundamental truth — we are perfect as we are, and there is always room for improvement.

FRIDAY 10

Believe in miracles

SATURDAY 11

Go with an open mind

SUNDAY 12

Dependability is the foundation of good character

AUGUST

There are going to be very painful moments in your life that will change your entire world in a matter of minutes. These moments will change you. Let them make you stronger, kinder, more compassionate. But don't you go and become someone that you're not. Cry – scream if you have to – then straighten up that crown and carry on.

MONDAY 13

Look out for the people you love

TUESDAY 14

Thoughts are seeds of deeds

WEDNESDAY 15

If life looks dark, turn on your own light

THURSDAY 16

Everyone just wants to be loved

EIGHT BRUTALLY HONEST TRUTHS YOU NEED TO HEAR IF YOU WANT TO GET YOUR LIFE TOGETHER

1 YOU MAY REGRET HOW MUCH TIME YOU SPEND ON SOCIAL MEDIA

Social media is actually making us all more disconnected than we've ever been before. It may be 'social' but it is still a 'medium' between you and others. So while you are able to 'communicate' with thousands, even millions, of people with ease, much of it is shallow. Don't use it as a substitute for real life connection and real life experiences.

2 YOUR REACTIONS CAN BE A PROBLEM

Yes, stuff happens, and you react. Sometimes you will get angry or upset by what others say or do. You can decide how much, and for how long, what other people say or do, is going to upset you.

3 FEAR KEEPS YOU SMALL

Stop playing small if you know you want to play big. Stop telling yourself "this is good enough" if you know deep down you would love to do, create, have and be, so much more, if you had the courage. The cost of taking that risk may be your long-term happiness.

4 YOU SHOULD ALWAYS HAVE ENOUGH MONEY FOR WHAT MATTERS

Money has to be earned. You trade your valuable time and talent for it. So why waste it on stuff that doesn't matter? Decide what is important and spend your money on that.

5 PEOPLE ARE GOING TO HATE YOU NO MATTER WHAT YOU DO

You can try and 'people please' your entire life, but no matter what, some people are going to dislike you. So rather than wasting your time trying to become someone you think **they** will like, spend your time becoming someone who **you** will love. You will have to live with yourself for a long time.

6 BLAMING ONLY MAKES YOU WEAKER

In the moment, it's easy to become the 'victim' and point the finger of blame towards a circumstance or other person. In the long term this doesn't work so well. The less you take responsibility for your choices and actions, the weaker you become mentally. Taking responsibility may come with some immediate repercussions, but over time, it builds a life founded on honesty, and it gives you real power to deal with challenges when they do arise.

7 PEOPLE DON'T THINK OF YOU AS MUCH AS YOU THINK THEY DO

From our perspective, the whole world revolves around us. We are all far more concerned with how others view us than by how we perceive them. So in a world of 7 billion people, you can relax and find peace in knowing that people are too concerned with themselves to give you as much as attention as you think they do.

8 NOT EVEN THE PERFECT RELATIONSHIP IS GOING TO COMPLETE YOU

Even people who seem to have found "the one," realise that true happiness comes from within. Relationships are an extension of our personal happiness and not the basis of it, so focus on strengthening the relationship with yourself and all of the others will follow accordingly.

93

AUGUST

If you want to build something great in the world, focus on the big problems and imagine the best solutions for these.

The secret of life is to fall seven times and to get up eight times.

Be a champion of the human spirit and its highest potentiality for good.

FRIDAY 17

Tomorrow is another day

SATURDAY 18

Good money habits will make you a fortune

SUNDAY 19

A good book is a great companion

I think if I've learned anything about friendship, it's to hang in, stay connected, fight for them, and let them fight for you. Don't walk away, don't be distracted, don't be too busy or tired, don't take them for granted. Friends are part of the glue that holds life and faith together. Powerful stuff.

Jon Katz

A friend is someone who knows all about you and still loves you.

You are the average of the five people you spend the most time with.

Jim Rohn

MONDAY 20

We all have all the time there is

TUESDAY 21

Learn to express anger without blame

WEDNESDAY 22

Do something nice for a friend

THURSDAY 23

Be great with people

AUGUST

I believe that everything happens for a reason.
People change so that you can learn to let go, things go
wrong so that you appreciate them when they're right,
you believe lies so you eventually learn to trust no one but
yourself, and sometimes good things fall apart so better
things can fall together.

Marilyn Monroe

No matter what people tell you, words
and ideas can change the world

Robin Williams

Any fool can know.
The point is to understand.

Albert Einstein

FRIDAY 24

You are exactly where you are meant to be

SATURDAY 25

Life is a wonderful voyage of discovery

SUNDAY 26

Take a holiday from your phone

You gain strength, courage and confidence by every experience in which you really stop to look fear in the face. You are able to say to yourself, 'I have lived through this horror. I can take the next thing that comes along.' You must do the thing you think you cannot do.

Eleanor Roosevelt

There is some good in this world, and it's worth fighting for.

JR Tolkien

Nurture your mind with great thoughts. To believe in the heroic makes heroes.

Benjamin Disraeli

The important thing is not to stop questioning. Curiosity has its own reason for existence. One cannot help but be in awe when one contemplates the mysteries of eternity, of life, of the marvelous structure of reality. It is enough if one tries merely to comprehend a little of this mystery each day.

MONDAY 27

Take up a new sport

TUESDAY 28

Set a new challenge

WEDNESDAY 29

Self-acceptance is essential for happiness

AUGUST

You can lead a human to knowledge, but you can't make him think.

Let us read, and let us dance; these two amusements will never do any harm to the world.

Voltaire

THURSDAY 30

When you say "thank you", mean it

FRIDAY 31

Silence is not always the best answer

A human being must have an occupation if he or she is not to become a nuisance in the world.

Of all sad words of tongue or pen, the saddest are these, 'It might have been'.

GOALS

FOR SEPTEMBER

Things I want to accomplish

Results I intend to achieve

Subjects I want to study

Movies I want to see

My dreams

Fairy tales are more than true: not because they tell us that dragons exist, but because they tell us that dragons can be beaten.

SATURDAY 1

There is more pleasure in giving than receiving

SEPTEMBER

When I'm wrong I'm learning
When I'm trying to figure
it out, I'm learning
When I'm right I'm learning.
I'm always leaning.
Life is my teacher.

There is nothing either good or bad, but thinking makes it so.

Shakespeare

WHAT WE LEARN FROM TREES

Stand tall,
Stand your ground,
Be flexible,
Stand alone,
Be strong,
Stand together,
Weather life's storms,
Be patient,
With time, you will grow.

SUNDAY 2

Your family is your first community

MONDAY 3

Do not be afraid to fail – it's all learning

TUESDAY 4

Face the reality of the world with courage

WEDNESDAY 5

Prepare for success or be prepared for failure

THURSDAY 6

'One day' is not so far away

Don't let one cloud obliterate the whole sky.
Anais Nin

I have just three things to teach: simplicity, patience, compassion. These three are your greatest treasures.
Lao Tzu

Folks are usually about as happy as they make up their minds to be.
Abraham Lincoln

Alone we can do so little; together we can do so much.
Helen Keller

SEPTEMBER

Love is always patient and kind. It is never jealous. Love is never boastful or conceited. It is never rude or selfish. It does not take offense and is not resentful. Love takes no pleasure in other people's sins, but delights in the truth. It is always ready to excuse, to trust, to hope, and to endure whatever comes.

Laughter is timeless. Imagination has no age. And dreams do come true.

Walt Disney

FRIDAY 7

There is only one you – ever

SATURDAY 8

Persevere – things worth having take time

SUNDAY 9

Face your fears head on

In spite of everything, I still believe people are really good at heart.

Anne Frank

MONDAY 10

Your life is not measured in 'likes'

TUESDAY 11

Greed will eventually bury even the lucky

WEDNESDAY 12

Perhaps what you are looking for is right in front of you

THURSDAY 13

Do something for someone less fortunate than you

FRIDAY 14

Imagine what it could be like to walk in someone else's shoes

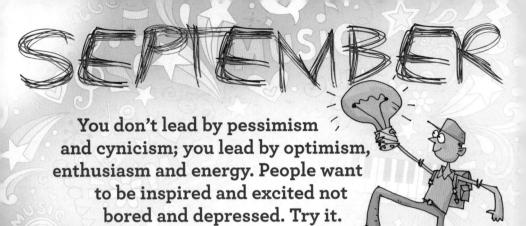

SEPTEMBER

You don't lead by pessimism and cynicism; you lead by optimism, enthusiasm and energy. People want to be inspired and excited not bored and depressed. Try it.

Patricia Ireland

SATURDAY 15

Be happy where you are with what you have

SUNDAY 16

Be open to new possibilities

Either write something worth reading or do something worth writing about.

Benjamin Franklin

All of the biggest technological inventions created by man – the airplane, the automobile, the computer – says little about his intelligence, but speaks volumes about his laziness.

Mark Kennedy

DON'T QUIT

When things go wrong, as they sometimes will,
When the road you're trudging seems all uphill,
When the funds are low and the debts are high,
And you want to smile, but you have to sigh,
When care is pressing you down a bit –
Rest if you must, but don't you quit.

Life is queer with its twists and turns,
As every one of us sometimes learns,
And many a fellow turns about
When he might have won had he stuck it out.
Don't give up though the pace seems slow –
You may succeed with another blow.
Often the goal is nearer than
It seems to a faint and faltering man;
Often the struggler has given up
When he might have captured the victor's cup;
And he learned too late when the night came down,
How close he was to the golden crown.
Success is failure turned inside out –
The silver tint in the clouds of doubt,

And you never can tell how close you are,
It might be near when it seems afar;
So stick to the fight when you're hardest hit –
It's when things seem worst that you must not quit.

Nothing that's worthwhile is ever easy.
Remember that.

MONDAY 17

It takes time to discover what you are capable of

SEPTEMBER

May you live every day of your life.
Jonathan Swift

To be yourself in a world that is constantly trying to make you something else is the greatest accomplishment.
Ralph Waldo Emerson

TUESDAY 18

Experience the thrill of winning

WEDNESDAY 19

Don't disdain what you don't understand

THURSDAY 20

The future depends on what you do now

FRIDAY 21

Make today a special day for someone

I've learned that people will forget what you said, people will forget what you did, but people will never forget how you made them feel.

Maya Angelou

Any sufficiently advanced technology is equivalent to magic.

Arthur C Clarke

SATURDAY 22

Global solutions need big picture thinking

SUNDAY 23

Your beliefs create your own reality

Life can only be understood backwards; but it must be lived forwards.

Søren Kierkegaard

I've learned from experience that the greater part of our happiness or misery depends on our dispositions and not on our circumstances.

Martha Washington

An eye for an eye will only make the whole world blind.

Mahatma Gandhi

SEPTEMBER

Do what **inspires** you.

MONDAY 24

Be willing to discover something new

TUESDAY 25

There is opportunity in every challenge

WEDNESDAY 26

Listen to the music in your heart

You don't love someone for their looks, or their clothes, or for their fancy car, but because they sing a song only you can hear.

Oscar Wilde

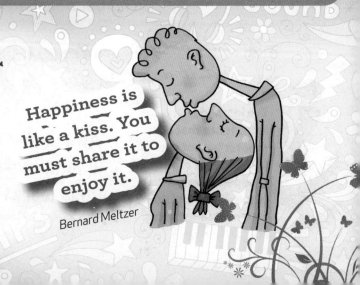

Happiness is like a kiss. You must share it to enjoy it.

Bernard Meltzer

*I have decided to stick to love...
Hate is too great a burden to bear.*

Martin Luther King Jr

To love oneself is the beginning of a life-long romance.

Oscar Wilde

One machine can do the work of fifty ordinary people. No machine can do the work of one extraordinary person.

Elbert Hubbard

THURSDAY 27

Be the enthusiastic one

FRIDAY 28

It's never the wrong time to do the right thing

SATURDAY 29

No one can be grateful and unhappy at the same time

SUNDAY 30

It's ok not to know the answer

GOALS

FOR OCTOBER

When you have eliminated all which is impossible, then whatever remains, however improbable, must be possible.

Things I want to accomplish

Results I intend to achieve

Skills I want to learn

Talents I want to practice

Most of the successful people I've known are the ones who do more listening than talking.

Bernard Baruch

Remember that the happiest people are not those getting more, but those giving more.

Jackson Brown Jr

If you are not willing to learn, no one can help you.
If you are determined to learn, no one can stop you.

In times of great stress or adversity, it's always best to keep busy, to plow your anger and your energy into something positive.

Lee Iacocca

If you want to change the world, start off by making your bed.
If you want to change the world, find someone to help you.
If you want to change the world, measure a person by the size of their heart.
If you want to change the world, stop being a snowflake and get on with it.
If you want to change the world, don't be afraid of what people think.
If you want to change the world, sometimes you have to dive in at the deep end.
If you want to change the world, be ready to swim with the sharks.
If you want to change the world, you must find strength in your darkest hour.
If you want to change the world, forgive your enemies.
If you want to change the world, start singing when all seems hopeless.
If you want to change the world, don't be the one that gives up.

MONDAY 1

Be the best friend you can be

OCTOBER

You can't have everything...
where would you put it?

I remind myself every morning: Nothing I say this day will teach me anything. So if I'm going to learn, I must do it by listening.
Larry King

Maybe life isn't about avoiding the bruises. Maybe it's about collecting the scars to demonstrate we showed up for it.

TUESDAY 2

Learn to take advice in the spirit in which it is given

WEDNESDAY 3

We can all do with a little help from our friends

THURSDAY 4

Wherever you go, show up as who you are

If the only prayer you say in your whole life is 'thank you', that would suffice.

Meister Eckhart

FRIDAY 5

The more love you give the bigger your heart gets

SATURDAY 6

There is enough for everyone

SUNDAY 7

You are responsible for all you say and do

Every single person makes a difference every single day. This takes people out of this helpless feeling of 'there is nothing I can do because the problems are too big.'

Dr Jane Goodall

The biggest adventure you can ever take is to live the life of your dreams.

Oprah Winfrey

OCTOBER

MONDAY 8

Make promises and keep them

Tomorrow is always fresh, with no mistakes in it yet.

LM Montgomery

Don't go around saying the world owes you a living. The world owes you nothing. It was here first.

Mark Twain

TUESDAY 9

Allow yourself to dream big dreams

WEDNESDAY 10

Be the architect of your own life

THURSDAY 11

Inspire others to do great things

Daring ideas are like chessmen moved forward: they may be beaten, but they may start a winning game.

Johann Wolfgang von Goethe

There are two ways of spreading light ... to be the candle, or the mirror that reflects it.

Edith Wharton

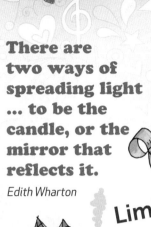

Limitations are only in our minds.

There is no psychiatrist in the world like a puppy licking your face.

Ben Williams

FRIDAY 12

Be a pioneer of the possible

SATURDAY 13

Everyone is deserving of respect

SUNDAY 14

Volunteer some of your time to help out

OCTOBER

A good deed brightens a dark world.

MONDAY 15

Take an art class

TUESDAY 16

Read about the lives of famous people

WEDNESDAY 17

Learn to dance

THURSDAY 18

Engage with great ideas

FRIDAY 19

Do what you can, with what you have, where you are

SATURDAY 20

You belong where you are

The best way to predict the future is to create it.

R Drucker

I learned this,
at least, by my experiment: that
if one advances confidently in the
direction of his dreams, and endeavors
to live the life which he has imagined,
he will meet with a success unexpected
in common hours.

Henry David Thoreau

Being the richest man in the cemetery
doesn't matter to me. Going to bed at
night saying we've done something
wonderful, that's what matters to me.

Steve Jobs

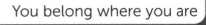

SUNDAY 21

Get on to the playing field

OCTOBER

**All we need is love.
But a little chocolate now
and then doesn't hurt.**

MONDAY 22

No athlete ever got to the winning podium without a good coach

TUESDAY 23

Be of good character – personality is often superficial

WEDNESDAY 24

Acknowledge your parents – they gave you the gift of life

THURSDAY 25

Share your fears with someone who can disappear them

FRIDAY 26

Don't hide your talents – share them with the world

Don't get discouraged. It's often the last key that opens the lock.

SATURDAY 27

Stand up for what is right

The real danger is not that computers will begin to think like men, but that men will begin to think like computers.
Sydney Harris

We delight in the beauty of the butterfly, but rarely admit the changes it has gone through to achieve that beauty.
Maya Angelou

If I have seen further, it is by standing on the shoulders of giants.
Isaac Newton

SUNDAY 28

Take advice from those who want the best for you

It takes a great deal of bravery to stand up to our enemies, but just as much to stand up to our friends.

JK Rowling

The great myth of our times is that technology is communication.

Libby Larsen

All of us could take a lesson from the weather – it pays no attention to criticism.

What you think of yourself is much more important than what others think about you.

Seneca

MONDAY 29 **BANK HOLIDAY**

Learn to cook

TUESDAY 30

Never take anyone or anything for granted

WEDNESDAY 31

Be gentle with the feelings of others

GOALS

FOR NOVEMBER

Things I want to accomplish

The seven
wonders of
the world:
   to see,
   to hear,
   to touch,
   to taste,
   to feel,
   to laugh,
   to love.

Results I intend to achieve

Books I want to read

Amount I want to save

It is a strange thing, but when you are dreading something, and would give anything to slow down time, it has a disobliging habit of speeding up.

JK Rowling

NOVEMBER

In order to cause a shadow to disappear, you must shine light on it.

Shakti Gawain

THURSDAY 1

Be great in small things

You can't outwit fate by standing on the sidelines placing little side bets about the outcome of life... if you don't play you can't win.

Judith McNaught

FRIDAY 2

Don't complicate your life

SATURDAY 3

Your drama is entertainment for others

SUNDAY 4

However good or bad a situation is, it will change

What you're supposed to do when you don't like a thing is change it. If you can't change it, change the way you think about it. Don't complain.

Maya Angelou

MONDAY 5

Walk your talk

Yesterday is history,
tomorrow is a mystery,
today is a gift,
which is why we call it the present.

TUESDAY 6

What you do with your life is up to you

WEDNESDAY 7

You cannot change other people

THURSDAY 8

Be the peaceful one

NOVEMBER

Don't talk about your walk let your walk do the talking for you.

FRIDAY 9

Be considerate of other peoples feelings

SATURDAY 10

When you forgive others, you also are forgiven

SUNDAY 11

Be a player not just a spectator

Every adversity, every failure and every heartache carries with it the seed of an equivalent or a greater benefit.

Napoleon Hill

**I have spread my dreams under your feet;
Tread softly because you tread on my dreams.**

WB Yeats

> Twenty years from now, you will be more disappointed by the things that you didn't do than by the ones you did do. So throw off the bowlines. Sail away from the safe harbour. Catch the trade winds in your sails.
> **Explore. Dream.** Discover.
>
> *Mark Twain*

MONDAY 12

It's a changing world, learn as you go

TUESDAY 13

Spend time getting to know your family

WEDNESDAY 14

Stay connected with what you love

THURSDAY 15

Parents just want you to be happy

FRIDAY 16

Get comfortable with hugging

NOVEMBER

Humanity is acquiring all the right technology for all the wrong reasons.

R Buckminster Fuller

Every man has his secret sorrows which the world knows not; and often times we call a man cold when he is only sad.

Henry Wadsworth Longfellow

Communication is an essential skill that you can learn. It's like riding a bicycle or typing. If you're willing to work at it, you can rapidly improve the quality of every part of your life.

Brian Tracy

SATURDAY 17

Do one thing at a time

SUNDAY 18

It's never the right time to do the wrong thing

You would never invite a thief into your house, so why would you allow thoughts that steal your joy, to make themselves at home in your mind?

MONDAY 19

Know you are valued

TUESDAY 20

Acknowledge a friend for being a friend

WEDNESDAY 21

It's ok be quiet

Those who cannot change their minds cannot change anything.

The human spirit must prevail over technology.

Albert Einstein

NOVEMBER

THURSDAY 22

Every performer needs an audience

FRIDAY 23

Say yes to new opportunities

SATURDAY 24

There is an artist in everybody

SUNDAY 25

Discover and express your own style

It is only when they go wrong that machines remind you how powerful they are.

Clive James

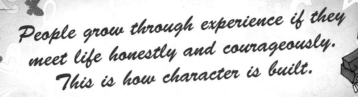

People grow through experience if they meet life honestly and courageously. This is how character is built.

MONDAY 26

Today is the tomorrow you created yesterday

TUESDAY 27

Don't lie to save your skin – you might lose your soul

WEDNESDAY 28

Forgive quickly and move on

THURSDAY 29

You know enough if you know how to learn

FRIDAY 30

Start an ideas book

GOALS

FOR

DECEMBER

Keep true to the dreams of your youth.

Friedrich Schiller

Things I want to accomplish

Results I intend to achieve

Nothing in the affairs of men is worthy of great anxiety.

Plato

Gifts I want to buy

People I want to acknowledge

The difference between who you are and who you want to be is what you do now.

Oh what a tangled web we weave when first we practice to deceive.

Sir Walter Scott

Christmas Gift List

1 <u>Buy a Get Up and Go diary for all my friends</u>

2 _____

3 _____

4 _____

5 _____

6 _____

7 _____

8 _____

9 _____

10 _____

DECEMBER

In the middle of difficulty lies opportunity.

Albert Einstein

Rowing harder doesn't help if the boat is headed in the wrong direction.

Every horizon that is reached reveals another, calling for a new adventure.

Don't look back, you're not going that way.

Put your thoughts to sleep, do not let them cast a shadow over the moon of your heart. Let go of thinking.

Rumi

SATURDAY 1

Everyone is entitled to their opinion

SUNDAY 2

Attitude determines everything

MONDAY 3

Laugh at bad jokes

TUESDAY 4

It's more fun to participate

WEDNESDAY 5

Don't believe everything you think

If you judge people, you have no time to love them.

Mother Teresa

For every minute you are angry you lose sixty seconds of happiness.

Ralph Waldo Emerson

It does not do well to dwell on dreams and forget to live, remember that.

JK Rowling

When I was 14, I came very close to becoming a gay teen suicide 'statistic,' but I then turned to music, my loved ones, and discovered that it does in fact get better.

DECEMBER

When you part from your friend, you grieve not;
For that which you love most in him may be clearer in his absence,
as the mountain to the climber is clearer from the plain.

Kahlil Gibran

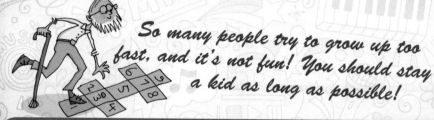

So many people try to grow up too fast, and it's not fun! You should stay a kid as long as possible!

THURSDAY 6

Singing is good for the soul

FRIDAY 7

Generosity will always be rewarded

SATURDAY 8

Take every opportunity to express your gratitude

SUNDAY 9

No matter what happens, stay connected with your friends

Darkness cannot drive out darkness: only light can do that. Hate cannot drive out hate: only love can do that.

Martin Luther King Jr

I speak to everyone in the same way, whether he is the garbage man or the president of the university.

Albert Einstein

MONDAY 10

The world is your oyster

My child,

I miss you something fierce,
but I knew I would have to share you with the world.
Take every moment by the tail and live full out! Remember to be
inquisitive, of integrity, kind, honest, fearless, open minded,
willing to make a difference, laugh at yourself, say I'm sorry,
practice empathy, work and play hard, and pay attention!
This will give you most of your dreams coming true.

Mom

DECEMBER

Our scientific power has out run our spiritual power.
We have guided missiles and misguided men.
Our hope for creative living lies in our ability
to re-establish the spiritual needs of our lives,
personal character and social justice.
Without this spiritual and moral reawakening
we shall destroy ourselves in the misuse
of our own instruments.

Martin Luther King

Good habits formed at youth make all the difference.

Aristotle

TUESDAY 11

Collect experiences not trinkets

WEDNESDAY 12

Start writing your autobiography – you may be famous some day

THURSDAY 13

Be willing to try

FRIDAY 14

Trust is a privilege you earn

SATURDAY 15

Don't be afraid to be different

SUNDAY 16

Learn the skills of good leadership

Technology is a queer thing. It brings you great gifts with one hand, and it stabs you in the back with the other.

CP Snow

It is not in the stars to hold our destiny but in ourselves.

William Shakespeare

Do not follow where the path may lead. Go instead where there is no path and leave a trail.

Ralph Waldo Emerson

DECEMBER

MONDAY 17

Get involved in fundraising

The best way to cheer yourself up is to try to cheer somebody else up.
Mark Twain

You only live once, but if you do it right, once is enough.
Mae West

TUESDAY 18

Cherish the freedom you have

WEDNESDAY 19

You have unlimited potential

THURSDAY 20

Change your thoughts and you can change the way you feel

> It takes courage to grow up and become who you really are.
>
> *EE Cummings*

DECORATE
yourself from the inside out.

Andrei Turnhollow

FRIDAY 21

Plan to live a big life

No dreamer is ever too small, and no dream is ever too big.

I wouldn't say I'm stuck in my adolescence, but I think, like a lot of people, I carry my teen years with me. I can still remember those feelings when everything seemed so intense and complicated and confusing.

SATURDAY 22

Money won't solve all the world's problems

SUNDAY 23

Be there for someone who needs you

DECEMBER

Kindness keeps the world afloat.

MONDAY 24 CHRISTMAS EVE

Cherish family time

Remember that wherever your heart is, there you will find your treasure.

Paulo Coelho

TUESDAY 25 CHRISTMAS DAY

Merry Christmas

WEDNESDAY 26

Good temper oils the wheels of life

THURSDAY 27

Be confident in who you are – you are unique

I like my new telephone,
my computer works just fine,
my calculator is perfect,
but Lord, I miss my mind!

Never be bullied into silence.
Never allow yourself to be made
a victim. Accept no one's
definition of your life;
define yourself.

Robert Frost

Christmas is not as much about opening our presents as opening our hearts.

Christmas is doing a little something extra for someone.
Charles Schulz

How dreary would be the world if there was no *Santa Claus!*

A Christmas candle is a lovely thing;
It makes no noise at all,
But softly gives itself away;
And quite unselfish, it grows small.

We are called to be architects of the future, not its victims.

R Buckminster Fuller

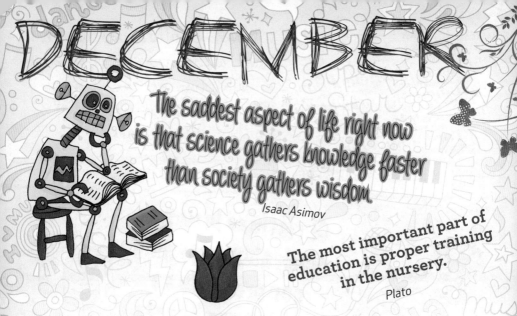

DECEMBER

The saddest aspect of life right now is that science gathers knowledge faster than society gathers wisdom

Isaac Asimov

The most important part of education is proper training in the nursery.

Plato

If you have no confidence in self, you are twice defeated in the race of life. With confidence, you have won before you have even started.

FRIDAY 28

Sometimes you can have what you want

SATURDAY 29

Nothing gets done if no one is bothered to do it

SUNDAY 30

Set a goal and make a plan to get there

Being a teenager is an amazing time and a hard time. It's when you make your best friends and your worst enemies. You get the best and the worst as a teen. You have the best friendships and the worst heartbreaks.

MONDAY 31 NEW YEAR'S EVE

Start to become the person you want to be

Give a girl the right shoes, and she can conquer the world.

Bette Midler

Promise me you'll always remember: You're braver than you believe, and stronger than you seem, and smarter than you think.

AA Milne

No one can make you feel inferior without your consent.

Eleanor Roosevelt

Never love anyone who treats you like you're ordinary.

Oscar Wilde

You cannot endow even the best machine with initiative; the jolliest steam-roller will not plant flowers.

Walter Lippmann

PARABLE OF THE
ROSE

A certain man planted a rose and watered it faithfully, and before it blossomed, he examined it. He saw the bud that would soon blossom and also the thorns. And he thought, "How can any beautiful flower come from a plant burdened with so many ugly thorns?" Saddened by this thought, he neglected to water the rose, and before it was ready to bloom, it died.

So it is with many people. Within every soul there is a rose. The beautiful qualities planted in us at birth growing amid the thorns of our humanity. Many of us look at ourselves and see only the thorns, the faults, the defects. We despair, thinking that nothing good can possibly come from us. We neglect to water the good within us, and spend all our time trying to get rid of the thorns.

We are all roses and thorns. The thorns are there to protect the rose. One of the greatest gifts a person can give is to reach past the thorns and find the rose within others. This is the characteristic of love, to look at a person, and knowing their 'faults', recognize the beauty in their soul. If we nurture the rose, we have no need to fear the thorns. The thorns will not outshine the rose in full bloom.

Our duty in this world is to nourish our roses and forgive our thorns.

Only then can we share the love we should feel for each other; only then can we fully bloom in our own garden.

Author unknown

You never really understand a person until you consider things from his point of view... Until you climb inside of his skin and walk around in it.

Harper Lee

I believe that imagination is stronger than knowledge. That myth is more potent than history. That dreams are more powerful than facts. That hope always triumphs over experience. That laughter is the only cure for grief. And I believe that love is stronger than death.

Robert Fulghum

It's the possibility of having a dream come true that makes life interesting.

Paulo Coelho

Somehow I can't believe that there are any heights that can't be scaled by a man who knows the secrets of making dreams come true. This special secret, it seems to me, can be summarised in four Cs. They are **curiosity, confidence, courage, and constancy, and the greatest of all is confidence.** When you believe in a thing, believe in it all the way, implicitly and unquestionably.

Walt Disney

Begin doing what you want to do *now*. We have only *this* moment, sparkling like a star in our hand, and melting like a snowflake.

145

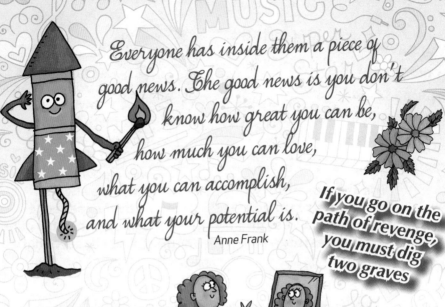

Everyone has inside them a piece of good news. The good news is you don't know how great you can be, how much you can love, what you can accomplish, and what your potential is.

Anne Frank

If you go on the path of revenge, you must dig two graves

What you think of yourself is much more important than what others think of you.

Seneca

Better to get hurt by the truth than comforted with a lie.

Nothing is more tiring and back-breaking than anger and stupidity. The relentless bitterness over what has or has not been done to us or for us. There is no harvest in that field, and the gardener ultimately dies in a dry patch of land, alone.

Tennessee Williams

DESIDERATA

Go placidly amid the noise and haste, and remember what peace there may be in silence. As far as possible without surrender be on good terms with all persons. Speak your truth quietly and clearly, and listen to others, even the dull and ignorant; they too have their story.

Avoid loud and aggressive persons, they are vexations to the spirit. If you compare yourself with others, you may become vain and bitter; for always there will be greater and lesser persons than yourself. Enjoy your achievements as well as your plans. Keep interested in your own career, however humble; it is a real possession in the changing fortunes of time. Exercise caution in your business affairs; for the world is full of trickery. But let this not blind you to what virtue there is; many persons strive for high ideals; and everywhere life is full of heroism.

Be yourself. Especially, do not feign affection. Neither be cynical about love; for in the face of all aridity and disenchantment it is perennial as the grass. Take kindly the counsel of the years, gracefully surrendering the things of youth. Nurture strength of spirit to shield you in sudden misfortune. But do not distress yourself with imaginings. Many fears are born of fatigue and loneliness. Beyond a wholesome discipline, be gentle with yourself.

You are a child of the universe, no less than the trees and the stars; you have a right to be here. And whether or not it is clear to you, no doubt the universe is unfolding as it should. Therefore be at peace with God, whatever you conceive Him to be; and whatever your labours and aspirations, in the noisy confusion of life keep peace with your soul. With all its sham, drudgery and broken dreams, it is still a beautiful world. Be cheerful. Strive to be happy.

Max Ehrmann

FOR MORE COPIES VISIT OUR WEBSITE
www.getupandgodiary.com

OR CONTACT US ON
info@getupandgodiary.com

Postal address: **Get Up and Go Publications Ltd, Camboline, Hazelwood, Sligo, Ireland F91 NP04**.

DIRECT ORDER FORM (please complete by ticking boxes)

PLEASE SEND ME:

The Irish Get Up and Go Diary **2018** ☐ **2019** ☐ €10/£9   Quantity ☐

The Irish Get Up and Go Diary (case bound) **2018** ☐ **2019** ☐ €15/£13   Quantity ☐

Get Up and Go Diary for Busy Women **2018** ☐ **2019** ☐ €10/£9   Quantity ☐

Get Up and Go Diary for Busy Women (case bound) **2018** ☐ **2019** ☐ €15/£13 Quantity ☐

Get Up and Go Diary **2018** ☐ **2019** ☐ €10/£9   Quantity ☐

Get Up and Go Diary for Girls **2018** ☐ **2019** ☐ €10/£9   Quantity ☐

Get Up and Go Diary for Boys **2018** ☐ **2019** ☐ €10/£9   Quantity ☐

Get Up and Go Travel Journal ☐ €12/£10.50   Quantity ☐

Get Up and Go Genius Journal ☐ €15/£13   Quantity ☐

Get Up and Go Student Journal (homework journal) ☐ €14/£12   Quantity ☐

Get Up and Go Heroes (all proceeds to charity) ☐ €10/£9   Quantity ☐

The Confidence to Succeed (by Donna Kennedy) ☐ €12.50/£10   Quantity ☐

Total number of copies ☐

P+P WITHIN IRELAND €2.50 PER COPY.
P+P INTERNATIONAL/OVERSEAS €3.50 PER COPY.

I enclose cheque/postal order for (total amount including P+P): _____

Name: _____

Address: _____

_____

Contact phone number: _____ Email: _____

For orders over eight items, please contact us on 086 1788631 / 071 9146717